PARSE

PARSE

RUTH BAUMANN

Black
Lawrence
Press

Black Lawrence Press

www.blacklawrence.com

Executive Editor: Diane Goettel
Chapbook Editor: Kit Frick
Book Design: Amy Freels
Cover Design: Zoe Norvell

Published 2018 by Black Lawrence Press.
Printed in the United States.

grateful acknowledgment to the journals which first published these pieces, sometimes in varying forms:

Crab Fat Magazine: Entryway
Devil's Lake: Belonging
Fog: Ars Poetica; Broadest Daylight; Lesson
Hardly Doughnuts: A Book Calls It Recognition Hunger; Alive with the Hauntings
New South: That Kind of History
Pretty Owl Poetry: Get Sober; Self-Portrait as Teenager; Why I Can't Daydream

additionally, part I was published in chapbook form from Black Lawrence Press, titled *Retribution Binary*

for lil Luz, who brought some light at the end of much dark discovery
(look how that always happens)

for the heart's endless capacity to regenerate

Contents

i.

GIRL

A body must reach an equilibrium regardless of its passions toward splintering.

Continue.

Imagine survival as a kind of farming.

Continue.

Are you sure?

THRASH [a study in wreckage]

I.

 The sun a spasm. Delirious with too much perspective. The girl moves forward. Sweat of course. Forward subjective of course. *Engulfed: verb:* state of being, state of impossibility. She's thinking of what she misses except she can't think. One thought crosses another like a car t-boning the future. Nesting dolls omnipotent. Gravel sticks to her toes, pinpricks little as a god memory. Something nags. *Here is a body put yourself in it & stay there & stay there & stay.*

THRASH [a study in wreckage]

II.

After a while the girl turns. To herself but outwardly. At her hands. Are these runaway hands? Runaway bones? A white bird overhead, *no* she instructs *no associations to surrender.* Visualizing a network of escape routes, hollow roads. A skeleton spread across the flatlands. Can it dance? What steps? Nothing but. She sighs. Onward. Like a whistle that brings the dark.

THRASH [a study in wreckage]

III.

On the road a wildflower. Purple as poison. Remember a vase on a table. Flowers. Nothing cracked, no morning light poured on red-edged pieces. Shatter a taught command. What is carved is not followed. Daylight daylight daylight. Her wrists movement factories. Memory unmanufactured. No bottle matters. Brightness like a bruise. A bottle though. How typical. *Go* she does *go further.* The narrative here known. Except for its thumbprint. She holds a lighter to her fingertips. Hail Mary to the temporary. Full of pain.

They say a delayed reaction to an alarming stimulus is a symptom of the body always in emergency mode.

She's weaving a basket.

Inside she'll place something borrowed something breathing something eating.

THRASH [a study in wreckage]

IV.

    Hands laid on the body lay still in the body. Ghost leeches parasites of rotten wanting. Ecosystem of the underworld. Closing her eyes a desolate landscape. This for comfort. Imagine an expanse mud-gray. Paled & drought-shrunk cacti like gravestones. In her head she skips. This is where she cannot be hurt. Nothing foreign drags her from herself. No hunt no hunt no sides. It has been a long time. So time no longer matters. Head up now she walks.

THRASH [a study in wreckage]

V.

Motion a waltz bereft of fear. No, saturated & bereft. She walks like an acoustic solo. Without instrument. Just wind. The mind of wind. Dreaming of not dreaming of the night the sky broke. Its hands robotic, grasping. A human cleaned like a mealbone. Once she was picked. In some cultures in some circles of hell, an honor. She wishes now on a full moon. Plucks the hours from her life like petals, terrified there may be no stem.

THRASH [a study in wreckage]

VI.

    Wishbones in the head a vortex. Clouds gathered at the nape. Storm a cheap medium. Dissolution, call it progress. Her sleep a glass wall against. Her body collected against an underpass. Rain watches. Keeps score, makes it up. When his eyes were big they were so. Glassy want-mongers million-tongued stupid pseudo-beast. Give a man dominoes & he will fish forever. She shivers. The gutting wasn't so bad. As was the living gutted. Emptiness the loudest papercut. But energy does not die. The raw blankness it feasts.

Do you want to keep going?

Do you feel guilty for being given the choice?

Red rover red rover
send hell on over.

THRASH [a study in wreckage]

VII.

Cart pulled to market creates the market. Dirt accumulating now, days tallied. A toenail breaks off like a mile marker. Destination thirst. Shadow long, shadow needy. Within her mouth many screams no mechanism. A car slows she does not. Supplies a game liquor plays with the flesh. *Curse*? Certain fires have an odor. Is she even visible. *When did you first know?* A hawk overhead. Circling nothing, starving itself. *If everyone dies who wins?* Death scholar. Maybe she's still pretty.

THRASH [a study in wreckage]

VIII.

If a web is cognizant. The poor spiders, all fucked. *Justification: nounverb: uninhabitable sphere.* The girl is not available. A lightbulb flickers in a passing truck. Fog today, like walking into a meditation of last breaths. Tornadoes shrunken & poised, in her for her. Give her this power. Destruction so wide though. A plain becomes a continent. The morphology of chaos. A hand emerging from quicksand her own she steps on it.

THRASH [a study in wreckage]

IX.

Aftermath one plus a hundred minuses equals. There are turnarounds. The girl doesn't. Red in the sky like crying baby skin. Pluck veins like a harp. Some sound. *Earthly pursuits* she thinks. Furious as a top spinning around itself its own sun. All planets demoted. Sailors pirates scoundrels delight. Sunset spawning, plummet plummet. When she unrolls dough. When she leaves by her side a rolling pin transformer. No stars just a cough in the fabric. The universe nodding, a shark bobbing in the swimming pool. *If you can't swim, kill.*

THRASH [a study in wreckage]

X.

    A snail on the back of a switchblade. Sing a song of disconnect. Devastation a reclaiming. One way of the world fear. A fence burgundy. How it impales landscape. Faster now, flight feet on. Sweet morphine of sleep, its feathers spread wide. A glance is enough. Asterisk *not*. Risk factor *a bow & arrow in outer space*. Risk factor *how cold the planets*. The girl asks for a little place to lay her head. She will keep walking after.

SCAVENGER

he wants

to tell you something

under a bridge

in your mouth

behind the pretty part

of your eyes

the dumb part

where you let

BLANK FACED MAN [a study in absence]

I.

Fascinated with the oblique

Aerosol head Blue head

Feet that believe in [redacted]

Feet that move towards [redacted]

He [redacted redacted]

Nothing escapes the flies

They see it all They get it

But he meant to come back

Not to anybody or anyplace Just

BLANK FACED MAN [a study in absence]

II.

Ancestrally who cares

When hands clap they expect a result

A sound An affirmation A value judgment

He digs a little hole Sticks an old self in it

But hollow   Is not   A cure

Have you asked?

A rake hunts the yard. First.

Then the approach of fire.

BLANK FACED MAN [a study in absence]

III.

Illness in light too A power in

Feet are not arrows Except inward Blah

blah Whole life from memory No—

Today he In a catbird's mouth

answers It chews It cries

BLANK FACED MAN [a study in absence]

IV.

Late morning light a hammer

An icebox A shotgun

He does not rise His need does

Load an arrow Never shoot

A birdcall A hollow

This is how one chases With

so little effort *Sludge* he mutters *Bring*

me sludge A paper plane swims by

Rain is a goal Is a throne

BLANK FACED MAN [a study in absence]

V.

Grimy hands grimy eyes

The mice eat stale cheese

The mice eat the mice

Between the toes no Beautification

No Idealization Just spaces

One serenade then One

lullaby then He doesn't set

anybody's table

Above the frame bells toll.

All blood out of

focus. Can you hear?

BLANK FACED MAN [a study in absence]

VI.

If the body is a crime Hell

His lips solemn His head whole

Her age is an appetite Wine on the ceiling

Which is good He'll send her

He'll send her to the ceiling Say a decade

BLANK FACED MAN [a study in absence]

VII.

But impossible improbable Impenetrable blame

A feast laid out For a blind tasteless eater

Yes/no Yes/no   Caesura

in delivery   In deliverance

Masks have a calling They open

a planet to a universe A light

turns on in a basement Pull the string

It turns brighter No/ no No /no

BLANK FACED MAN [a study in absence]

VIII.

After months After bottles shine

their broken light like new faces

After the crowd After the faultlines

lick their sleeping bodies Doesn't

a junky curl into a comma

No sentence Madness origami

Universe situated in a fireplace

O no promise O no hymn

Long walk home So stay

Long night home Do you know

where your handler is?

BLANK FACED MAN [a study in wreckage]

IX.

Hologram Hologram   Have a field day

Burn the blunt The spoon The repetition

of a single song all afternoon   Burn the brain

into a hook   Cups catching the rain

Pour them back to the sky   Burn

trust in any mystics   His hand lulls

across dead grass   The earth is stacked so thick

BLANK FACED MAN [a study in wreckage]

X.

Stars pooling like blood No milk

in the whiskey Because the world

is carrion A vehicle A predictable

He will stuff his throat with cherries

It's not hate It's smaller than that

Nobody get a broom Not on

his anti-watch

ii.

Entryway

Little fire flows from the head. Daylight is innumerable.

I sat in a box for one lifetime. I built it a surrounding room that was
also a box. I painted the windows, I placed
one man blocking the door, then
another, then
another.

SELF: An object that knows itself operates from a principle of joy.
SELF: I do not know myself.

What do you want to say?

I wish years didn't pile like bricks.

When I was small I had a particular daydream.

I imagined an act of violence. A character perpetuating it on me. I had a
gun to my head, or a knife to my throat. Usually abduction. But I'd find
my way out, wounded, only to be rescued by a man. Or he'd rescue me
when I called him from the phone in the motel while the attacker was
unconscious.

The fantasy always ended there. I had no idea what happened past
rescue.

You see, if I was strong enough, if I was tough enough,

I would be loved.

It's common, the image projected onto a blank face.

But the image lies
distorted.

SELF: A pool of water named *Origin*.
SELF: A silencing gun placed in every expanse that lives.
SELF: [speaking at a cellular level]

[self-inflicted self-portrait, age 27]

Just promise me you're not going to hurt yourself, because I need to get back to work now.

Sweet mother let me plant you a field of weeping willows mother.

Daylight hello. Will I ever know what to do?

Space & age are not recriminations. Voices are.

TRANSCRIPT REDACTED

December & wildflowers still bloom the driveway. I am free to breathe within & without my body.

GUIDE: You are free!

SELF: [twists]

Scrape

In time a large mouth appears.

From it a river a battalion of rivers.

I make new names for my parents I build them
paper boats I force them
away.

*You're pretty but you're
annoying. You're
crazy let me
back to my absence
of inner life.*

Shiloh was a battle. Gettysburg. Antietam.

So what of
a teenage daughter downing all the pills
she can wash down with the liquor &
the cough syrup & the
hunger o god the primal

                                    hunger nobody picks up on
                                        between tirades—

                                               does it count,
                                               is it anything?

I cover my floor in dead petals, I don't pick them up, I live
against wishes.

Rebellion is still an act of
the owned, I know.

A voice absconded.
A voice rustic, painted
rusted, hollowed
& burnt out, left by the creek
where the child hides
to snort glass & think
about what she's done,

how her body is to blame for the wishbones
she/it becomes.

Danger sign! Up ahead a movement
in the psyche.

What if I told you

I will choose to be an orphan? My tongue
tastes new berries. I pick
a green-grassed universe.

SCENE: rampant.

SCENE: red red red red red grey.

I spent my life apologizing, bleeding, sticking
a skin up my nose.

Family you spent I spent then

then I put your ghosts into the soft pulpy heads
of a thousand crimson balloons
& I released them.

Nobody watched.

Growth Dialogue

The splitz to be seen.

One brightly colored scarf instead
of veins please.

THERAPIST: *If you are disturbed it doesn't mean something is wrong
with you.*

PATIENT: *Even the moon pulls its dead close.*

THERAPIST: [moves in chair]

Small the child just wanted. Larger,
still
still.

PATIENT: *My keepers are incapable.*

THERAPIST: *Glue has many sources.*

No ceremony for first steps.
No wreaths hung about a neck.

PATIENT: *Send flashlights.*

Modus Operandi, Revised

It's growing, understand, the giant mouth, the one that operates at intersections

It's mostly in my head but sometimes it lives in my lungs

Lungs I pretended were heart for so long

Listen: water makes a sound even when undisturbed

Sometimes that sound is stamina Sometimes it is me

because the rivers of charcoal of ash of family ashes

because the long-fingered men with the weight

because the actual pull the vacuum the child I asked

because some species their eyes change color when they're blind

but mine were always blue

when I let go of the men everything came back

I lay in a fetal position for months   I became estranged

I realized it wasn't just the obvious attacks on me by others it was the years

of dropping me into a bag full of sand demanding it cover my thoughts & words

the children in adults is made of fear.

but in several ways I am done.

ghosts cannot eat me

I come to you now bearing enough teeth

iii.

Ars Poetica

when my father said *it's your fault*

you were raped the black in his eyes
was big enough to put a fist in

but instead I chose colors I chose

flags I cooked so much poison
I set a place for myself

at my own table

Considering Childhood

I pull surviving from my throat like scarves like
that good bathtub brewed magic *God,*
sit up straight I am full of interference
My brain a scratch-off ticket But
God, the dead don't have to mourn
inside the living I have a small cat now
She has only seen me sober We are
capable of this *God, do you have*
the stomach God, I have
some answers for you The stars
dribble overhead Flakes of perfect
celestial vomit

Lesson

They say *don't idealize*. But
the wind wears so many masks

& I keep taking it to bed. If
I call myself a practitioner

do you need an image? A pool
of tepid water, crying

to every raindrop
I love you, not really dreaming

more than once.

Alive with the Hauntings

Art not being a way into the stars.
Art being a way out.

For so long I fell asleep thinking.
Then earlier

snuck up. It came at me with open
palms. It gave me choice:

six thousand miles to the center
or two steps. Either way,

I had to greet the center. So
raw, so disinterested in insanity!

Childhood grief is like a stone
worn around the neck, I've

heard. Also I've heard
a bird cry in the middle of the night

like it needed dawn *now*. & who
was god to argue?

Holiday

I meant to be enough.

I covered my body in water &
commanded *expand*.

I laid meat in the forest, I invited
the hunters & hunted alike.

We're having a party the invitation read.
Bring your real face &
the one you wear.

A chorus showed up. *Call us*
the insatiable they said.

They opened their mouths & sucked
sound away.

Saga

Actually nothing can take the place of light.

I step forward. From the other side of the lineup I choose myself.

This one has a price tag attached say the bars. How strange they can talk.

But this has never stopped me before.

Prayer for Fists

There are so many conditions with the enemy.

When there is weather, I must take responsibility.

I am the one human on a planet full.

I cast my voice into canyon after faceless canyon.

I am your only mother the enemy says, the slur subtle.

The moon drops behind clouds from pity.

The enemy pleads for old behaviors. It pushes me to walk first,

so the winter wind breaks on my face, unaware

that the cold shapes me new, thank god, all new.

Dear R

Glued into stillness. A finer attention to sounds: inhalation of minutiae.
You are a morning alone by yourself. I want to talk to you about your
habit to make everything beautiful.

There's actually nothing wrong with it.

Dear R, *your whole life is finding the user's manual
to yourself,* says the therapist's handout. *Memory
is mood-dependent.*

The men have gathered their hooves,
pushed themselves off a horizon. *You can think
differently*, the handout promises, next to a drawing
of a smiling brain.

Dear R

I want to call you & tell you I've learned thirty new lessons about quiet.

I know you. I want you
to stop dreaming yourself trapped in your abandoned refrigerator, to stop
leaving the porch light on in the Florida November midnights.
All it illuminates are the animals that forgot to hibernate.

R, you of the ill-advised emotional flailings on couches
with men built from pendulums. Honey,
they love your skin's impressive deafness.

R, I wish you could love yourself for other,
for instance
this conversation you have with your cat:

You: *I did it again, I swore a blood oath with a ghost.*

Cat (unimpressed): *Who wasn't born in a vat of blame?*

You: *Whatever, watch me breathe.* Time passes
in the foreground.

You: You: You:

Get Sober

Little long legged birds run on the beach

while I practice the absence of imagination.

Or, the difference of. Can light shine

in a tunnel where a man stands, mouthing

I love you, each word a racing train? [No.]

I sunburn my arms & go home alone,

thank god, I cannot stand the replaceability.

Finally I Bought Myself

Because for how long my low price?

Red hung at the windows, the sheets, the

tears in my lips. O Lord at the altar of fruit

& delusion I have laid I have lied I

said *you* then *you* then I forgot

the question's cost. Wildflowers, now,

without poison. Wildflowers & that little space

between breath & pain, I bought myself

that real estate.

That Kind of History

I want to chisel new tools from anger, from body, those slow wrong
feasts. When I was myself I

struck a deal: I knew the handcuffs, but only by mind, that faulty, spider
of a compass.

Gods of Unreasonable Reality I ask. I own merely the language of fight
but I ask for that chair

across from my actual self ten years ago. The stars like ringworm in the
sky but I ask. The stars like

little selves disassociated from dark beds but I ask. I close my limbs I do
not belong to what I've

given myself to, time & time again, my *this* self a soil tilled & tilled, raw
earth red & without core:

do you see, I'd ask, if I got that chair. *Do you see what you don't have to do?*

A Book Calls It Recognition Hunger

Repackaging, I present
a thousand winters. I imagine
really the same scene over
& over. Can the external
provide? *Are you even asking?*
But I've lost the throat
to ask, the appetite to answer.
O littlest little self, you have
no more idols. Snow falls
like sugar. I cut apart my tongue.

Letter to Self/ Family Lineage

Weird little art compound can you house something other
than a junky addict addict addict can you
spell a new word can you exasperate a new
inability to feel   I am so tired
of transactions   of asking for & receiving
the old language   later I will place
a clean dish in a clean cupboard   I read a poem once
that called one thing *bone-white* but here everything is.

Why I Can't Daydream

From inside the sun, does everything look bright
or is it just boring? No man can save me. I understand
& now I approach my head

the way a hunk of meat approaches
a fly.

I Used to Be A Romantic

I threw sword after sword into my eyes.

Are you returning? I asked the shadows, figuring they must
be angels. *What else do you want
to lose?* they responded, voices light &
airy as the emptiness

the air
in my arms.

I split the throat of flowers. I demanded a list of names. I ran
my body down the fence until I bled myself

to another side.

Narrative

This is the apple

This is the bottle

This is the mouth

This is the center of gravity: we call it *loss*, for short.

This is the head

This is the darkness it emerges from: we call it *home*, for short.

Then, after a while, I began to practice breathing. First it was short &
then it was.

Self-Portrait as Teenager

If your thoughts are not valuable

If the water bowl is full of liquor If
you lap
lap If you are untamed &
moderately claimed If

your feelings are problems If
you stuff towels around the door
& lift the furniture

to find bumps of crystal If
everybody is an empty hall & you

are voice echoing If lightning
can strike over &
over If you don't know

what to do with the spots
where it hasn't burned the grass

Like A Child Shoved Into A Tunnel

Mothers & Fathers,
you misnamed misdesigned swallowers
of actual light: give me my heavens
of angers, let me hold angers like antlers
charge into your frostbitten night: some families
say *love,* others say *cleave*, push until

Forgiving Those Who Do Not Repent

Tired is an inadequate country full of inadequate spears.

No
I won't ground this spatially: did you
ever hand me a map you hadn't spit-scrubbed blank?

Fires
heal wildlife in every season,
mother, father, you plain half-songs of broken-backed birds.

I imagine loss, its million ideas.

I wish I could write you better.

No
I wish reality, now, floods & floods of reality, now,
& you just twigs from a fallen tree on the crest of some debris-laden wave,
just that,

go home,
let me forgive the water instead.

Freedomscape

Inquisitive thought is good
says a side character

Is light fire or a point
of entry or all of the above I ask

A thousand swallows overhead
Sometimes I am one

The primaries hand me
shovels made of spines

But it's not so dark When
I dig I make room

Terms

Child-within is
a phrase & I'd like

to not be angry about it.
I'd like my disappointment

to be cavalry, a fleet
of wild buffalo. Instead

thinness. Instead I hold
my own scalps &

toss them at the feet
of the ghost men

with their ghost words &
those little black vacancy

eyes. Ancestors I follow.
Ancestors I follow. Such

sweet craters I've
been gifted.

Belonging

The first time I put meth up my nose I thought *Oh*.
Well that's a line crossed. Of course
it's that easy, becoming more than I thought possible,
in any direction—*Oh*. I have this theory,
that hell & family slink in like that, not
on baby cat feet, but
in one normalized *Oh* after another.

How birdsong

used to signal hangovers, that tightening of the rope. Do you remember?

You used to help me. You used to say *I love you, you're so smart.* Then

you sat at the table & handed me every skin you couldn't shed.
Remarkably easy to distill into a liquor! & The birds

became representative for this wide open space, how fucking desolate
an afternoon of stillness. Because stillness has this tendency to reveal.
Because, father,

we raise ourselves in the wild if we have to. Or, in your case, we raise

the stakes. I've been sober, father, & not only that. I've been scrubbing,
father, I've been getting rid of all these images

of rescue—

Young

Once I drank

whiskey in a

hotel room with

my mother in

the mountains of

West Virginia &

we watched a movie

about Johnny Cash

& I snorted speed

in the bathroom.

Repeat repeat. Once

I asked god

her alibi. Repeat

repeat. There's never

enough water to

submerge a world

fully. I have

bowed at the

feet of the

commandments of abyss.

No, I was

not startled. Ever.

Broadest Daylight

I let go of one language.

I threw it into a pool.
It threw me

into the world, then.

Over & over I ask. *What more*
can I do to speed
through emptiness?

This is real sobriety says
the crowd of birds, herons
maybe, flocked & free
around a Florida winter's blue-eyed sky,
able to love
themselves

or at least to peck
a dead creature's eyes
comfortably.

Acknowledgments

Gratitude being the primary emotion—gratitude (& compassion) being the desired default state(s)—so much gratitude here:

Thank you to all my family, widespread.

Thank you to Anna Rose Carson, Jen Charles, Sharon Hartman, Netty Lehn, Margaret Mauk, Tara Mae Mulroy, Dyan Neary & Diana Stoen for being *some* of my chosen sisters (I could not possibly ask for more love, humor, wisdom & weirdness than I get with y'all); thank you to Jon (Jawn) Knapp for being the best (much younger) brother there ever was; thank you to Kaveh Akbar for being a chosen brother (& poetry hero); thank you to Merrell McQueen for being the best kitten grandfather imaginable; thank you to Brandi Nicole Martin for being Lou Lou's godmother & also an excellent poet & friend; thank you to Bill Sharpe for letting me adopt you as granddad (& for the fashion inspiration); thank you to Jane Dwyer Lee for being so generous with her wisdom, love, simplicity, & direction.

Thank you to so many of the talented teachers I've been gifted: John Bensko, Andrew Epstein, Barbara Hamby, Jimmy Kimbrell, David Kirby, Sonja Livingston, Dennis Moore, & Diane Roberts.

Thank you to so many of the talented poets & writers I can't believe I get to know in real life: Ruth Awad, Erin Belieu, Paige Blair, Brandi Bradley, Kelly Butler, Maari Carter, Damian Caudill, Anne Champion, Alexa Doran, Kat Finch, Katie Ford, Matthew Henriksen, Tiffany Isaacs, Paige Lewis, Zach Linge, Colleen Mayo, Kat Moore, Jon Mundell, Erin

J. Mullkin, Brian Oliu, Alex Quinlan, Jayme Ringleb, Emily Skaja, Jake Syersak, Karen Tucker, Kina Viola-Cain, Marty Viola-Cain, Dillon Welch, Marcus Wicker & Josh Wild (& more, more than I could fit here).

Thank you to Kit Frick & Diane Goettel & Black Lawrence Press for being the absolute dream publisher. I could not be more grateful & awed by you.

Thank you to every kitten I've fostered (especially Luz, Skunk & T.Rex) & every person who has loved & adopted those kittens. Thank you to my permanent cats: the elders Autumn & Julia, & the second generation babies, Lou Lou & Joy.

Thank you to the activists who inspire me. Thank you for all your courage over fear. Thank you for all your noise—may you never stop.

Thank you, an assorted thank you, for the support, kindness, & love of: Erin Adams, Rana Alsiro, Ryan Ash, Shea Atkin, Lauren Chapman, Emily Ferron, Chantal Fortin, Anna Herrington, Ashley Howell, Alexa Kelly, Matt Kelly, Carrie McPeters Kramer, Terel Lasiter, Lakey Love, Elizabeth Cameron-Luzader, Miranda McLaughlin, David McNeil, Sarah Shelton, Rosalyn Stilling, Kera Twomey, Shelly Wilkerson, Karen Williams, Paul Zammit & Pipon Zammit.

Thank you to my parents and my grandmothers.

Thank you to the world for being a place I won't give up on. Thank you to poetry for giving me a home in that world & in myself. Thank you to the light that's always there, somewhere, somehow.

Photo: Kenneth L. Johnson

Ruth Baumann is a PhD student at Florida State University & holds an MFA from the University of Memphis. She is also a co-editor of *Nightjar Review*. She's the author of four chapbooks: *A Thousand Are Poeticas* (Sixth Finch), *Retribution Binary* (Black Lawrence Press), *wildcold* (Slash Pines Press), & *I'll Love You Forever & Other Temporary Valentines* (Salt Hill). Poems are published in *Colorado Review, Sonora Review, Sycamore Review, The Journal, Third Coast* & others listed at www.ruthbaumann.com.